What You Do With Days

Acknowledgments

Some of these poems first appeared in *Thumbscrew, The North, Impossible Horizons* (1995), *Only So Much* (2011), *A Sheffield Miscellany,* and *Sheffieldish,* a chapbook published by Cochlea Press in 2016, and launched that year at the Broomhill Festival. Other poems were displayed on hoardings down the Moor in 2011 during the rebuilding of Sheffield Market.

Other publications by Michael Glover

Poetry:

Measured Lives (1994)
Impossible Horizons (1995)
A Small Modicum of Folly (1997)
The Bead-Eyed Man (1999)
Amidst All This Debris (2001)
For the Sheer Hell of Living (2008)
Only So Much (2011)
Hypothetical May Morning (2018)
Messages to Federico (2018)

Others:

The Trapper (2008)
Headlong into Pennilessness (2011)
Great Works: Encounters with Art (2016)
Playing Out in the Wireless Days (2017)
111 Places in Sheffield That You Shouldn't Miss (2017)
Late Days (2018)
Neo Rauch (2019)
The Book of Extremities (2019)
Thrust: (2019)
John Ruskin: an idiosyncratic dictionary (2019)

As editor or contributor:

Memories of Duveen Brothers (1976)
Goin' down, down, down: Matthew Ronay (2006)
Between Eagles and Pioneers: Georg Baselitz (2011)
Robert Therrien (2016)
Monique Frydman (2017)

What You Do With Days

Sheffield Poems

Michael Glover

Copyright © Michael Glover 2019

Cover painting © Mick Rick
Photographs on pp. 13, 19, 23, 27, 30,
32, 57, 65, 73, 77, 88© Mick Jones
Thanks fellas.
Other photographs © the author and Steven Kay

Cover font: Limelight Copyright © 2011 Sorkin Type Co
(www.sorkintype.com),

The Walking Man by local sculptor George Fullard (1923-1973)
stands outside Sheffield Winter Gardens, forever on the move.

www.1889books.co.uk

For Ruth, my lodestar

Contents

45 Coningsby Road

Back Yard Scene	1
A Right Old Back Door Scene	
Everything That Happens in Our Back Yard	2
The Gas Lamp at the Top of Blyde Road	
In the Kitchen	4
Legs Recovering Sharpish	5
Early Morning	
Bath Night	6
A Tasty Bit of Cod	
Cheeky Little Aporth	8
Captain Custer on the Sofa	
Being Poorly	10
That Man	11
The Gossipy Gob of Our Next Door Neighbour	12
Back From Holiday	14
Billy Graham Crusade, Sheffield, 1964	
and how it played out down our street)	
Lovely Things in Fir Vale, 1964	
Rough Talk	15
All Up in the Air	
Are You Stopping?	16
Aunt Edna From Llandudno	17
Uncle Ken	
Off to the Locarno, 1967	18
Boom	
Safe as Houses	20
Best of All	
The Death of The Sunbeam Cinema,	
Fir Vale, Sheffield 5	21
In a Sheffield Attic	22
Old Blues Lyric Crooned	
in a Sheffield Teenager's Bedroom, 1966	

The Carpet Layer from Liverpool Courts
    my Mother at 45 Coningsby Road   24
Drunken Domesticity   25
Sid Comes Back From the War, 1945
The Demolition of 45 Coningsby Road   26

Firs Hill School

One Hundred Lines at Firs Hill Primary School   31
Writing on the Blackboard
Better, Better, Better...   33
In the Headmaster's Study
Footie   34
Yellow Weeds

43 Green Oak Road, Totley

Marital Bliss   39
Going Round the Lump
Night and Day   40
Dorothy Collects Her Pension at Totley Rise
A Cup of Tea in the Kitchen   41
That Second Cup of Tea   43
All You Ever Need in Totley
Teeth   44

Out and About in Sheffield

On a Park Bench at Millhouses   47
Maud and Jesus
Time on Your Hands   48
Roe Woods
Double Sheffield Portrait   50
An Old Mester Leant Against a Wall on Osgathorpe Road   51
My Pal
Herbert's Story   52
A Front Room in Pitsmoor   53

Sheffield Tobacco Smoke on the Tram Into Town	
Saturday, 11.55 p.m.	54
New Pink Trainers	
Big Head in the Sportsman	56
Old Folks	
At the Milk Bar in Fargate	58
That Big, Gosterin' Woman	
in the Sportsman, Barnsley Road	60
Walking Man	62
Staring at Her Picture	
To the Moor	64
Sour Puss	66
Leave Me Alone	
The Accident	67
Something Precious	
Blackpool Promenade	68
The Dangers of Blackpool Rock	
Hope	70
Walking Through Days	
All the Time in the World	71
Middle-aged Bachelor in Profile at the Window	
Big Girls	72
What Gets You Going	74
English Teacher Walking up Barnsley Road, 1967	
The Pain of Separation	75
Barretta Street (down Owler Lane way)	
His Street	76
Just Don't Try it	78
The Best Necklace	
Coach	
Girls Everywhere	79
Early Bird	80
Not a Word	
Laughter	82
What's it All About Then?	83
Greyhound Racing at Poole Road	
Biding His Time	84

Just Not Noticing   84
Gormless   86
All-Talk
Emily   87
Kiddies   89
Revenge
Losing the Winking Kind   90
What it's come down to...
Sheffieldish   91

Endgame

In the Palliative Care Ward at the Northern General Hospital 97
Saying Goodbye to Mother
City Road Cemetery, Sheffield   98
Safely Elsewhere   99
Dorothy and I on Wincobank Hill   100

A Personal Note About This Book

These poems about the city of my birth and growing were written over a long span of years, perhaps about thirty in all. The last of them turned up very recently. That is how it is with poems. They just turn up - like uninvited guests. Or like old friends. Somewhere between the two. How fresh the past comes to seems as you grow into your life! Almost more vividly present than the present itself, which can be a little hazy and undependable by comparison.

This book is divided into various sections. The first three demand at least a modicum of explanation because they are particular locations, two to the unfashionable north-east of the city, and one to the more prosperous south-west, where muck never hung in the air or besmirched freshly laundered sheets. 45 Coningsby Road in Fir Vale is the small terraced house where I lived until I was nineteen years old. These poems are set either in that house or within its immediate neighbourhood. That little terraced house was small, cold, damp and delightful to a child who knew nothing else. Its staircase up to the two bedrooms and attic upstairs was terrifyingly steep, which was fun. Mountaineering in all but name. A lot of people lived there with me, and when they rowed, as they often did, the racket of those voices in contention made the walls bow outwards. Almost.

I went to school at Firs Hill Primary. I was a dutiful boy, quiet, none too assertive, often in fear of big, brassy lasses, and towards the lower end of the second division when it came to skills involving legs and feet. 43 Green Oak Road Totley, where my mother and her husband went to live after the purposeless demolition of our side of Coningsby Road - it was demolished in order to facilitate the widening of Herries Road, which never happened - was quieter, and nudged up against magnificent countryside. It was also a small, tuneless box of a place to me, without much spirit or even a modicum of mayhem. I missed the cramped dampness of Coningsby Road. And so the poems in this section feel a little more lonely and less convivial. Most of the rest of the book finds me going into town with my collar up, listening in to what other people say to each other, observing what they do, how they walk or caper or booze or frolic, and generally sniffing around and enjoying everything that the big city of Sheffield promises when it brazenly winks back at you.

Michael Glover 2019

45 Coningsby Road

Back Yard Scene, 45 Coningsby Road, Fir Vale, Sheffield 1958

My mother ran and whisked the washing in.
The soot flakes fell, black snow from a grey sky.
The beer barrels came trundling along,
With surly men in aprons by their side.

The shelter that had kept the Germans out
Stood staunch and ugly by the lavvy doors.
We crept in there to hear our voices shout
Out swear words, tell real ghost stories, lose balls.

An outside lavvy's not a bad thing though,
Especially when the greens make you feel sick.
I stuffed them in my cheeks like hamsters do,
And shot them out in bits. The water flicked.

A Right Old Back Door Scene

You don't have to say anything.
You've said more than enough already,
So much so that I switched off for most of it.

If you want to, just do it.
Why bother about what *I* think?
You never did before.

There's an open door in front of you,
or at least there will be
when you open it.

Don't expect me
to do it for you, will you,
you lippy bugger.

Everything That Happens in Our Back Yard

Rent man comes by wi' his pencil and book
From John Smith the Brewers
To note down payments.
Papa 'ands it ovver at t' door.
No smilin'.

Coal man bustles down t' yard
Wi' his face all black,
In his cap, 'eavin a sack,
Flashin' his white teeth at mum.
She smiles back, sharpish.

When gypsy cart stops in t' street
For owd clothes,
We get pegs in exchange.
They're good for ends of noses -
And for peggin' on t' washing line
Strung across back yard
Me sister's saggy blue school knickers.

The Gas Lamp at the Top of Blyde Road

When the gas lamp comes on,
we'll be out there again,
making the usual racket -
hoola hoops, tag, hop scotch,
riding our Christmas bikes.
There will be no stopping us,
will there, tonight?

In the Kitchen

On t' floor by t' roll-top secretaire,
There were an owd blue flock rug.
Bits used to come off it when you pulled.
Lift up corner (if you dared)
An' you'd get slimy silver fish dartin' everywhere.

Toastin' fork stood on its prongy legs in t' grate.
Stick toast on t' prong ends...
Next thing, toast's black as death wi' chokin' smoke.
Fire spat out bits o' coyl an' all.
Nan said you 'ad to watch it.

Bath neet were great, every Thursday.
Zinc bath heaved up from t' cellar.
Blankets coverin' t' clothes 'orse
In front o't' fire
To mek it private.

When t' kettle whistled,
There were a deafenin' racket.
Umpteen pans an' buckets
O' pourin', boilin' watter.
Stick a toe in too smartish,
You'd whip it straight out again, bawlin'.

Sittin' in' t' bath, starin' at fire,
Nowt but yoursen,
Behind that clothes horse,
Just wallowin', in a dream, legs thrashin',
In a big tub o' steamin' watter...

After you came yer sister.
Same watter,
Wi' a bit more added.
Bein' 'er,
There were scent an' pongy stuff after.

Legs Recovering Sharpish

She took those steep stairs up
all of a puff, one step at a time.
Oh, how she moaned and groaned!
Her legs just weren't up to it these days.

So they fixed her up a bed
in the front room instead,
facing the street,
where nebby neighbours could peer in.
No thanks for that!
Legs got a second wind:
up in a jiff.
It were just like magic.

Early Morning

Someone is waiting to ignite the fire.
The fuel's all there – coal, faggots, paper spills.
Someone's stooped over, coughing, by the range,
An old man, with black fingers, peering up
Into the dark interior above,
Its soot-caked sides... Is something really there?
He's heard a scuffle. *Summat's not quite reyt...*
Up goes that hand, a third time, reaching round...

All of a rush, it comes, pink, blotchy-black.
He cups it in his palm. It's warm as toast.
Mabs! he shouts up. There's scuffling upstairs.
All of a rush she comes, and takes the bird.

Bath Night

How many times do I have to tell you
to take that spoon out of your mouth
when you're sauntering round this kitchen?

Don't you know that if you were to trip and fall
you'd knock half your teeth out
and probably put your eye out an' all?

Take it out, will you, this minute,
you little devil and a half,
and don't go pulling faces at me
as if I'm something not quite right.

Now just sit down, will you,
and finish off your eggs and bacon.
It's bath night tonight, mester man,
and you stink to high heaven.

A Tasty Bit of Cod

I'm nobody you'll ever know.
I live in Osgathorpe Road,
at the Barnsley Road end.
That's me there, going round the lump.

Every day I do it – past the allotments,
even when it gets quite chilly.
I wouldn't not do it, oh no.
It keeps me healthy.

I'm nobody you'll ever know.
I've queued behind you once or twice likely.
I don't need much though –
a bag of hot chips, salted, with a tasty bit of cod on a Friday.

Cheeky Little Aporth

Marbles roll round and round
in the backyard grate
for as long as
you flick them.

Then it rains again,
and you go back into the kitchen
to watch mother up to her
all-white wrists in flour and pastry.

If you smile in a certain way,
and keep on smiling,
and put your head under her arm
as she works with her fingers,

you get wet sloppy sweet bits of dough
plonked down and then pointed out with a finger jab
that never go in the oven.
You also get called *cheeky little aporth*.

Captain Custer on the Sofa

It's ten o'clock, and you're still in your pyjamas
on a school day. What's up with you, fella-my-lad?
The only thing you're fit for, I reckon,
is staring at Captain Custer on horseback
in that big book of yours on the sofa -
good job Christmas came early! -
with you lying stretched out
all hot and floppy and achy,
waiting for the doctor,
who'll know in a jiff what you've got.

Mum's crashing around at the sink.
Then she brings you yellow Lucozade in a glass
that fizzes right up your nostrils
just before the doctor comes in,
glasses nearly tumbling off his nose end,
and pokes around and about your skinny chest
with something cold and rubbery,
and then scribbles something in a flash
as he's frowning down and breathing heavily.

You'd better get that made up at the chemist.
He presses it to her. He calls her Dorothy
on account of the weekly anaemia injections
with that big, fat needle in his consulting room.
You have to wait outside for ages, flicking through old mags.
Mum nods, all serious,
just as Captain Custer lets another Indian have it.
On horseback you can always move so fast
on a school-day morning just past ten o'clock.

It's rubbish feeling rubbish.

Being Poorly

Times goes ever so slowly
when you're poorly.
You just lie there,
head all hot heavy,
flexing your fingers weakly,
with the fast world
racing ahead of you.

Now and again
someone switches on a smile,
wipes at your forehead

with a cold, damp cloth,
then shakes a head.
Most time they just get on with it,
clatter-banging around you.
They don't stop when you stop.
They get busier than ever,
and you can't flex
even a finger end's length
to make them slow down to your pace.
You just have to pull a sad face,
grin a tearful grin, and bear it.

That Man

When that man over there says nothing,
he says a lot.
He says more than enough.
He's still there when I look.

I tell him he's gone.
I shout it out loud.
But he's not.
And I'm there too,

waiting for him
waiting for me.
No, I'm not.
I've run off,

dodging, breathless, stumbling
through the trees of Roe Woods,
panting fit to bust,
with my breathing so noisy,

running, running,
yet never quite out of reach,

and still going hell for leather
until... here I am again,

in my own bed,
in my bedroom,
and there's nothing else around me
but this slow circling of good things -

the alarm clock, that Bible,
and the map of America at last,
with Yellowstone Park and Yogi,
held fast by coloured pins
directly above me.

The Gossipy Gob of Our Next Door Neighbour

Mrs Aidy weren't exactly
What my mother'd call a lady.
All she ever had to fill her insides
Were a packet of fags, and vinegar sandwiches
In bread as thick as a house-side!

But was she some strong!
She once lifted me straight through their window
When her daughter locked her out in a temper.
But that was the least we had to sort out.
They'd lob the dinner plates when they really got going,
And once, after one of them had sent the other flying off a chair,
My mother found Mrs Aidy coming to
                        at the bottom of the cellar stairs.

I think she deserved all she got.
After all, would you take it sitting down
If your mother kept the kettle on the hob
Just for the pleasure of steaming open
Your sweetheart's letters
So that she'd something to fill her gossipy gob?

Back From Holiday

She came back from being away with Millie
all pink in the face and legs
and giggly silly.
She was full of it -

nights out every day,
boys, chocolates, fun fair rides,
the lot, all at once - fab, fab, fab, mum! -
spending money, money, money.

What were *you* doing then
when I were enjoying myself?
I didn't even bother to answer.
She's never been into stamps.

Billy Graham Crusade, Sheffield, 1964
(and how it played out down our street)

Mrs Lockin's jumped on Billy's gospel train.
Fags in the dustbin and drink down the drain.
Hands off the mincer and up with the blind.
Cycle the fat off your great behind!

Lovely Things in Fir Vale, 1964

Chopped pork from the beeroff.
Lemon and Lime from Latham's.
Burns a hole in your pocket on Sat'day, does
Friday night's savings.

Rough Talk

I don't want any sweet talk from you.
You never meant what you said any road.
You were allus pullin me leg.
You were allus laughin at me behind me back,

because of who I was,
because of where I'd come from.
You wouldn't have been seen dead wi' me
if a better bloke had come along.

I'm still here though, aren't I?
I've seen to your every need.
I give you house-keeping on a Sunday.
Every so often you get a new pair of shoes.

What else do you want?
Do you think that I'm made of money?
Why are you allus givin me that funny look?
Don't you know you're God's gift to me, you soft 'aporth?

All Up in the Air

This is the very last time I'm goin' to say it.
You just stay out of this room. It's private!
I'm putting a lock on the door next time you do it.
I don't want you pokin' your nose into my things.

My belongings are all neat and tidy.
Yours are all messed up, like a heap of old rubbish.
If you throw my letters up in the air again,
I'll skin you alive, you little bugger.

Are You Stopping?

Where you going then?
Will you be gone long?
I need to know.
I might need me medicine.

I know it's just here.
I can see it.
I can even rattle it.
You watch me.

I might forget it though.
I might just nod off
and not know
what time it is.

What time is it any road?
Have you just come back then?
Or are you off out again?
What you got your coat on for
if you're stopping?
I hate to see you with that coat on again
when you're supposed to be
here with me in this kitchen.

Aunt Edna from Llandudno

I never thought much about her.
She was just a relation in the comfy chair,
big floral hat plonked down beside her,
fingers drumming.

She said a lot about nowt much,
but I never listened.
My mother tidied up furiously around her.
Nanny was kinder.

When she passed away,
she left a little present for me,
a ten bob note,
for Mikey, it read.

Quick as a jiff I spent it
on nothing I can now remember.

Uncle Ken

He barely spoke.
He wrote instead, with a pencil,
in a little red note book,
bendy, that he kept in his back pocket.

Instead of getting cross,
he went out to the pub,
but not for long.
His finger ends went yellow from smoking.

I loved him more than I said.
I got my own little note book and pen.
I even wrote about him now and again.
He made this poem here happen.

Off to the Locarno, 1967

You look daft in them shoes.
You're gonna break your neck in them.
Is there a nest in that bee-hive hair-do?
I wish I'd never had a sister like you.

Elvis allus looked stupid in them shiny suits.
You just don't get me, do you?
I'm playing this guitar cos I want to.
I'm bein' loud cos it's loud music.

Why don't you go out an' stay out for a change?
That dress needs takin' in, mum.
It's baggy where it's supposed to be tight.
Eh up, she's left her lipstick behind.

Boom

Some days I just can't stand it,
the way nothing every changes,

the way you're there again,
standing just so,

the way the houses are all
squeezed up against each other

row upon row of them
up the hillside...

I'd like a bomb to drop
on all of them. Boom.

I fancy playing accordion
on a side street in Moscow,
with icicles for finger ends.

Safe as Houses

Please God keep me safe
in the usual places -
where this street meets
the main road
at the traffic lights,
and with her here, forever,
in this kitchen.
That's where I want to be
most of all,
safe as houses
inside this house
of patched up bricks
and crumbling mortar.

I don't have to venture far.
Just so long as you
keep me safe here.
Just so long as
I can pretend
you've heard me.

Best of all

Best of all is this attic room
where you shut yourself away
with books and thoughts and biscuits
and read poetry by Shelley
until you fall asleep,
fully-clothed...
Best of all is this attic room
with a skylight corner
from which to see
grey-tiled rooftops

and to hear machinery whining
from that little factory
where you never go,
but glimpse, side-on,
as you hurry up Herries Road
once in a while...

Best of all is to be up here
dreaming of what might be,
and never to go down there
into that hell of stupid talking -
that kitchen of blazing lights,
bustling bodies and reeking bacon -
about nothing that really matters.

The Death of The Sunbeam Cinema, Fir Vale, Sheffield 5

Nothing's so sad as buildings you once loved
Being brought down by a ball on a long chain.
That's how it was with our old cinema,
The only Sunbeam brightening up Fir Vale.

A wonky line of ragged, laughing kids,
We'd queue on Sat'day mornings in the rain,
Waiting for Captain Marvel and his cloak,
Clutching a bag of sweets and some small change.

It fell in a great pother of brick dust,
With that ball thumping at the topmost walls.
I'd hated seeing it boarded up and dead.
My mum whisked me off shopping to Page Hall.

In a Sheffield Attic

Step inside these pages.
Warm your hands at the fire of these words.
Outside it's winter.
The poor are clamouring to be heard.

Lean down and listen.
A sweetness is rising up,
the cadence of sentences
surging along as they must.

Outside darkness has fallen.
Juddering pinpricks of yellow light
are searching for someone somewhere.
Inside everything is all right.

They are bearing you to a kingdom.
You are sleeping. You are also awake.
Someone greets you with infinite tenderness.
You are master of all you survey.

Amidst all these houses there is your house
on an unremarkable street
where someone waits for coal to be delivered.
It is much later than you think.

Old Blues Lyric Crooned
in a Sheffield teenager's bedroom, 1966

Sweet Jesus laid him down on an ample feather bed.
He surely was a tired boy now on account of
   the blood he had shed.

I didn't think one thing
To the stain that he left on my sheet.

They say that man's blood does endure.
And I say that Jesus is sweet.

Sweet is a funny old word
That means nothing, but something to me.

Sweet was the kiss that I gave.
And sweet was the kiss he gave me.

But was he alive when he kissed?
And was it a real thing I felt?

And am I alive to tell this?
Or is this a holler from hell?

**The Carpet Layer from Liverpool
Courts My Mother at 45 Coningsby Road**

Late in the day I'm thinking of you.
I scent your breath in my nostrils.
I touch your finger with its rings.
So many rings, from such far away places.
It seemed a marvel to me then, you and me.

Late in the day I'm thinking of you.
You're with me now as we waltz the room.
Your footsteps seem so light on the linoleum.
Your voice is breathy and peaceful,
Sweet as this boiled sweet I'm sucking on.

Late in the day I'm thinking of you.
I begin at the beginning,
With my arrival at your door.
I'm a little awkward that day,
Shifting the shortie mac from chair to chair.

You point down at the carpet.
I bring out the stanley knife.
I pare at its edges, doing my best
To make the straightest line of my life.
And you are looking on, tasty as a chocolate eclair.

Drunken Domesticity

One man shouts in a room, to huge effect.
A small child cringes – down to finger height.
A woman flings an arm out, desperate.
The man withdraws. His boots ring down the night.

A child's tear glistens on a red, pulped cheek.
The woman chinks a cup, so delicate.
Loud, bitter breath is fogging up the streets.
The child is in his bed, and doesn't sleep.

The man stabs at the lock with hazy aim.
He swears, then hammers. Swears. It opens up.
Pale light falls on the lino's greasy grain,
And on that doormat too, which reads GOOD LUCK.

Sid Comes Back from the War, 1945

When he came back on VE Day, I didn't recognise 'im.
Mrs Moorhouse came out from next door, an' she just said:
He's back, Dorothy, Sid's back.
He's left his bags at neighbour's. Gone for a drink.
I fainted when I saw him.

He were completely black from bein' in Burma that long.
He had these long ginger moustaches, waxed at both ends.

No glasses either.
He'd had malaria, diptheria.
He often shook after that.
It were frightenin'.

I didn't want to know him.
He wanted to tek me away wi' 'im, but I didn't want to go.
Then, when I got pregnant wi' you, he said:
Whose do you think *he* is then? He's certainly not mine.
He wouldn't acknowledge you.
He were a reyt bugger, that one.

The Demolition of 45 Coningsby Road

The long, slow defiance of cold bedrooms.
The perfect plausibility of stairs.
The pent embarrassment of shuttered closets.
The waiting and the waiting of a chair.

The unexpected heartache of small windows.
The pleasurable fever of the leaf.
The nasty little promise of a knife's edge.
The consequence of air, whirled into grief.

The nature, lackadaisical, of scissors.
One hot, remembered corner, all my life...
The coming and the going and the coming.
The filling and the emptying. The blight.

The tearing down of walls. The strokes of hammers.
The fissuring of glass. The shapes of mouths.
A sledge's dirty burial, with ashes.
The gradual retreat. The candle out.

Firs Hill School

One Hundred Lines at Firs Hill Primary School

Summat takes me back to that yard
Where I see little kids through a winder
Jostlin' wi' a ball, and Bill,
Who's starin' in at me, mouthin'
Where've you tekken your 'ook to, then?
I'm doin' them lines, my look says.
He nods, runs off.

<u>I must not kick a ball</u> at window panes.
I write it once, and then again, again.
My hand's all numb. Outside they're goin' mad,
Beltin' that ball across the yard and back.
Parkie's playin' a blinder, weavin' in an out,
Shorts rolled way up...

It weren't my fault though,
I'm thinkin', frownin' to mesen,
Parkie just lobbed it
Reyt onto my foot.
It just sprung up from me toe end.
Weren't nowt I could do but look.
Honest, sir.
Ball just bounced up. Next thing: smash.
An' that were that.

Writing on the Blackboard

Writing your name's no easy business.
You never forget what it sounds like,
But when tacher puts you on the spot,
It often just slips off the edge of your tongue
When you poke it out to help you think
In front of the blackboard.

Better, Better, Better...

Every day I get a bit better.
Teacher says so.
I'm up to T now.
I were only at B a week last Thursday.

That's why I'm playing out now,
Belting this ball against this wall,
Because I'm coming out reyt at last.
I'm not that useless little pillock any more.

In the Headmaster's Study

All he had when he turned out his pockets
were some fluff and a hankie
hard and grey as dried snot
could ever make it.

He shrugged and just waited.
That's all he could do.
Just because he was so big
that kids bounced off him

didn't mean he was to blame
for every titchy mardy arse
that ever fell flat on his face
in a school playground.

Footie

When Michael Parkin,
socks rolled down to his ankles,
dribbled a blinder in the playground,
and then tucked the ball in
between two heaps of muddy school blazers,

he just stood there, hands on hips, staring back,
and wondered why his legs had frozen stiff
just when they needed to slide out
and tap it off his toe end
to stop it happening.

Yellow Weeds

Weeds are that tough.
They don't mind buses
spewing out muck,
noise or general malarkey.

Trodden on,
they perk back up,
dust off the dust,
especially when it's sunny.

Nobody owns weeds.
Nobody bothers with them.
They're kept out of gardens with tables.
They just go where they want to.

I wish weeds were flowers.
Then folk might love them.
I were a big yellow weed in a school play once.
I got hissed off the stage for malarkey.

43 Green Oak Road, Totley

Marital Bliss

At the crabbed end of that long bed
The man's head lies. Readying himself
Against hard pillows, two of them,
He opens the book with careful hand.

The one beside him's already asleep.
From time to time she grunts,
Throws an arm, even speaks.
There's no sense at all in what she says.
He ignores it, reads on.
His hero's dying. He'll soon be dead.

At one by the clock, off goes the light.
It's always been like this, he thinks –
Staring into the dark a little while,
Feeling the bulk of her there,
Re-fighting that hero's fight.

Going Round the Lump

When the best of words fail me,
I go out to look instead,
inspecting how the grass is growing
on the front lawns up Green Oak Road,
tyre-tracked for the sake of good patterning,
or how the kiddies are squealing their resentments
at some crusty, stiff-limbed neighbour,
formerly of the Parachute Regiment,
who has locked his front gate forever.

Humdrum life,
broken up into manageable bits such as these,
you are always so refreshing.

Night and Day

He locked the front door top and bottom,
with a special screw for the bathroom window.
He never answered after seven,
door nor phone.
It was no good shouting.
The telly always shouted louder.

Come morning time, he's out at seven,
pottering about in the back garden,
same old grouch
yet a different person somehow,
champion now,
cracking his face smiling.

Dorothy Collects Her Pension at Totley Rise

Make it as far as the shops if you can.
No one'll stop you.
Fiddle with your purse at the greengrocer's.
Smile weakly at the delivery man.

When you reach the post office,
listen closely when she asks after your health.
You'll hear a word or two.
Then slide the money, in a cellophane bag,
away from her kindly hand.

Back at your own kitchen,
you'll count it all out again with the curtains drawn,
as you always do,
the pence, the florins, the old soiled notes.
Under the bed it will go, under the floor boards.

Then you'll attend to a clatter of saucepans,
and, after a dab or two to remove the gravy
from the corners of your mouth,
a long, slow afternoon
will be stretching ahead of you,
with a window to be watching out from,
and a good bit of sighing to be done.

A Cup of Tea in the Kitchen

The tea looks blockish, like wood,
In this tall glass cup.
I sip at it gingerly.
There's always too much.
It tastes like liquid iron might taste.
I almost give up.

The tea, thickly brown,
goes down in a slow, turning swirl
like water down the plughole of a sink,
Partially blocked.
I swallow on it, hard.
I sift it through my teeth.
It's liquid gristle, liquid meat.

'Do you want another, love,
or will one be enough?'
'Plenty, thanks, mum.'
I slip across to the sink
with the cup half veiled behind my hand,
Tea half drunk.

That Second Cup of Tea

You would have wished me sleeping perhaps,
with one arm tucked under my head,
and, seeing that,
you would have tiptoed away again,
and back down the stairs
without even jangling saucer and cup.

No matter, you would have said to yourself,
as you slipped side-on into the kitchen,
elbow leading,
no matter, you would have said
as you trickled the tea down the sink,

the lad needs his sleep
after that much hard work.
A strong cup of tea can always come
second time around.
It stands to reason.

All You Ever Need in Totley

Now he was reduced to it because he lacked her,
he decided it was as much as he had ever wanted
of the quiet poshness of Totley, to be sitting here
in the kitchen, facing the window,
with the gable end opposite in full view,
at which, just occasionally, a child would belt a ball or two.

There might even be a wave, and one back,
should the child ever spot him
raising his arm to make the gesture -
seldom, it has to be said,
seldom because dog tiredness
so often overtook him.
Otherwise, it was much about endless cups of tea and

chocolate eclairs at the munching hour of five,
yes, cups of tea at all hours,
strong, with three heaped teaspoons of sugar,
and fry-ups daily – sausage, bacon, eggs,
and fried bread done with the rest to soak up the fat,
and, on a Sunday, gammon, well boiled on the Saturday night,
and then left to settle underneath the tea towel,
to be there in the fridge come Sunday
almost as a surprise. That was as much as
he really needed now she was no longer alive
(as the wise world understood it.)

Teeth

He never came back from going away.
No amount of window-gazing helped,
nor thinking about him.
She just got on and did other things instead -
pottering about the garden
or getting a job settling
old folks into their beds
without overmuch fuss or shouting from matron.

Not that it helped much.
He always came back again in his own quiet way,
every time she closed her eyes
or switched off the light in their bedroom at night,
in a favourite suit (to tell the truth, the only smart one),
or with the trilby tilted just so (jaunty),
opening the car door like a proper gentleman,
and closing it again, firmly, without slamming,
and then smiling through the glass
just to show off the whiteness of his brand new teeth
after he'd tapped with his finger to make her notice.

No one could have made her get rid of them.
Let them just try calling her barmy.

Out and About in Sheffield

On a Park Bench at Millhouses

If you stood here and looked,
you'd see what I see,
not much, granted,
but more than enough for me -

a park with swings,
kiddies gostering,
water slopping out of blue buckets,
a roundabout for feeling giggly dizzy,

and, now and again –
if you were really lucky - a peek of sunlight.
How much more do you need then?
You tell me.

Maud and Jesus

It goes and comes,
through thick and thin, pleasure does.
I've never counted on it.
You just do your bit, daily,

dusting off the plants,
sweeping the carpet,
dubbining the step,
boiling up lites for the cat,

then go to bed
and think of Jesus,
how he needs you, steady and ready,
for when he drops in, any day soonish.

Time on Your Hands

He gave away the time on his hands
to another old man, one bench along,
in Gleadless Park,

and the man just sat there like souse,
doing nothing with it,
just staring down,

as if to have time on your hands,
even as a gift, meant nothing to anyone
who'd ever failed to notice.

Roe Woods

It is likely to be here once again that I find you.
This is the spot where you would always be sitting,
Shoeless, arm carelessly thrown back, peering idly
     into some clump of bushes.
We shared the pleasures of this drifting woodland.

It is likely to be tomorrow that I shall chance upon you.
You were always waiting for me tomorrow, then tomorrow,
     ever ready to give me your signal.
It was always a smile that you gave me, barely noticeable,
And yet I saw it, at no matter what a distance
     I might happen to be standing.

It is always here that I shall remember you.
It is raining today, adding some weight to my shoulders.
I lick at the drops with my tongue's tip, I smile,
     and I idle.
I am, as ever, expectant for you. There is no one here
     to prevent you.

Double Sheffield Portrait

She owned him lock, stock and barrel.
She owned the trousers that depended from his shanks.
She owned the gloves that muffled his creaky fingers.
She owned every last part of him, with small thanks.

She owned him lock, stock and barrel.
She owned his whistle, reedy, across the pond.
She owned the saliva in his mouth, and the roaring
   in his chest.
She owned the busyness of his words,
   and his small and finicky infuriations.
She owned the pots and pans that hung amongst
   the tools in his dank and lonely shed.
She owned his life, such as it was.

He owned her, lock, stock and barrel.
He owned how she glared at him long and long,
   like motor car headlights left on in the night.
He owned the gristle in her voice, and the stamp
   of her ungainly hoof.
He owned her buttocks, her ears, those tufty sprigs
   that showered out from each ear.
He owned every last part of her, and he made of her
   what he could.

An Old Mester,
Leant against a Wall on Osgathorpe Road

It were called lonely talk, the way he spoke to himself
  when you happened along of a morning.
In fact, it were a small miracle of lost or dying truths:
How the hedges were left untrimmed, bird-favouring,
  before the council took over;
How the boys would saunter along for an hour or two,
  no bother at all, to the local school;
How the lessons would all fall away so quickly –
  like water drying off a sun-beaten back;
How nothing would matter except what seemed to matter
  and then, sometimes, not even that.
His face would hang there, nodding,
  like an apple in a water butt,
Ruddy as an apple's too, with that fixed, glazed smile,
and a bit of slavering at the edge of the mouth...
I would tousle his hair with my hand – there was still
  more than enough of it!
He would raise his stick in mock-ferocity
And then, oh so slowly, let it fall back, dreamily.

My Pal

He's good as gold, she said,
patting him on the head.
He just stared ahead,
saying nothing, whimpering.

When she led him off, I wondered:
why did my pal get like that? And then,
when a van hits you in the road,
does that always happen?

Herbert's Story

I didn't go anywhere.
I just stayed put here, digging in,
in the same old house,
with the fussy bits of half-timbering
mum once said were so smart.

Other things changed all round me.
The people, for example,
always polite, pleasant, quietly discrete
when you speak.
The roof fell in opposite
because the landlord chose not to care.
Now there's a new-build over there.

I've still got the same garden shed,
and the same TV we always had
when mum was here.
I don't need much more.
Like St Francis before me,
I give bacon fat to the birds.

The pub got sold.
Its sign's still swinging,
a piece of nonsense riding the air.
You can't smell beer on breath round here,
not any more.
There's no Saturday night loudness neither.
Little lads run about as if they were on hot coals
when there's evening prayer.

One by one the trees got lopped.
They were a danger to all of us.
The roots made pavements erupt.
They could have fallen on a car!
Luckily, Roe Woods' still there to wander in.

You'll find loads of trees, more and more of them
since the air got cleaner.
You could say there's lots that's better.
What's more, I'm still here. I'm a fixture.

A Front Room in Pitsmoor

Little habits die hard:
The way she twizzled with her hair
   when the adults weren't watching;
That sweet and lazy song she used to sing beneath her breath;
The fall of her coat when she dropped it on the chair.
I would have given anything to see her again –
To watch the way she stared at me when she was pretending
   not to look;
To smile back at her after she'd turned away;
To have one of our chats when he'd left for the afternoon.
I'd give a reward to anyone who gave her back to me.

Sheffield Tobacco Smoke on the Tram into Town

Bitter and acrid,
It'd catch at the back of your throat,
all that manly puffed out tobacco smoke,
when you sat on the tram's top deck, lookin' down,
proud to be nearly drivin',

with coins janglin' in your pocket,
and the whole of Sat'day morning in town -
from Lady's Bridge, on up through Haymarket to Fargate -
spread out before you
like a fat slice of Wilf's chewy parkin.

Saturday, 11.55pm

Likely as not I'll make it to the street,
Then vomit on the pavement, sour and sweet,
The lot of it, quick-shovelled in, now out,
With all that ale, Niagara-belched, in one great gout.

Now I feel better, champion you might say,
My eye as level as this wall you'll see
Beyond the window, as I storm through the door,
Bent over, ready for man's task once more.

New Pink Trainers

Her mouth is so big
you can hear her in Rotherham.
I'm not kidding.

I'm going to tie her to a post
to keep stray dogs away.
She'd terrify them.

If she wasn't my sister,
I'd even love
watching her showing off

her new pink trainers
at the bus stop.
She'd never ever be embarrassing.

Big Head in The Sportsman, Barnsley Road

This big man came and dropped his head
beside my head on this rough old floor.
I'd never seen such a weight of head –
like a massive piece of furniture...

This big old man with his rough old hands
picked my head up and spun it round.
Did you make this one? Oh no, I said,
my mother made it, the silly clown.

He bounced my head with his big old hands
like a ball bounced on a rough old floor,
And all this time, his big old head
bobbed, as if nothing'd please him more.

Old Folks

They just potter around all day, old folks,
doing nowt much to speak of.
You see them when you're speeding along.
If they see you first, they can sometimes raise a stick.

I've got loads of times for them.
They'll tell you things you'd never know. For starters,
how to whittle a stick just so,
or what death was like once, and how they'd dodged it.

Sometimes they just stare down, thinking,
eyes going so far back
you could never ever reach them.
You're far too young and cocky to even notice.

At the Milk Bar in Fargate

She has the mellowness to satisfy me,
But not the easy swing of the legs.
She has that high-toned way with the napkins,
But not the dampish curl at the brow.
She has a way of tilting the glass when she fills it,
But the stubbed fingers are somewhat lacking.
I love her for the much that she is and the little.
And all for the asking.

She has that calm way of assurance
When the fevers demand attention.
She is quick with the poultice, the compress
When life is leaking out at the corners.
She can raise up, lie flat, swivel,
And generally re-arrange the parts that are
    falling to pieces.
I blow her kisses for all of this.
And I also remark those knobby swellings
    at the elbow.

She is my stanchion, my pillar, my hanging lamp.
She is the formicaed table which smooths towards me
On its bright brass castors.
She is the story, endlessly told,
    of our joys and triumphs in the making.
She is a perpetual spillage of words,
    bright and bubbly-babbling.
She is also those ankles.

Now have a **HORLICKS**

Horlicks

HOT or COLD

That Big, Gosterin' Woman in the Sportsman, Barnsley Road

This woman, she took me,
and she gobbled me up.

She had this great big voracious gob,
and she stuck me inside there,
and made a hearty meal of me.

I would have protested
had I been able.
I would have stood up on that table
and said: I am not like eggs,
bacon and a tablespoonful of beans.

I am not here to do your bidding.
To eat me would be quite obscene.

But she had already done it
by the time I opened my small gob.
Mine was just a gob lying on its own there
Without even a face to surround it
by the time I steeled myself to say it.

It was just a small man's working gob
inside the slobber and the dark
of all that red heave of hers....

Walking Man

My friend the walking man
just keeps going, on and on, walking.
Well, why not?
Collar up, head blade-thin, jaw set,
why stop when you've once started?

The world's not right as it is,
it's all skew-whiff, off kilter.
The rich get ever richer,
the poor ever poorer.
And where are we in all of that?
I'm a walking man
with much determination.
Let's go arm in arm, friend.

Staring at Her Picture

When she died for the first time,
I cried all the tears out.
When she did it again, I lost patience
by getting drunk and smashing up a car.

Knowing now that she'll do it again and again,
and often when I'm not looking,
makes me live in a world
too strange to be spoken of,
a world I want no part of, not really.

To the Moor

a toast to its coming resurrection
as the shoppers' paradise

Down this gently sloping street,
down this mecca of old-fashioned shopping pleasures,
let my feet go tripping and skipping.
Let old shillings jangle in my pocket
and new notes come spilling.

Let me say those names over to myself –
Pauldons, Atkinsons, Roberts, Redgates –
as I dart into first one and then another, ever singing.
Oh glorious palaces of bygone enchantment,
you who hold out to me forever
promises of new coats, and ever sheerer stockings!

And when I mount the bus back, weary, to Pitsmoor,
laden like a mule with bags in abundance –
too many to be carried, yet still I carry them –
toys for the kiddies, a new coat for mother,
a trilby for father...

I ask you, O Moor ever more-ish,
to stay vivid in my heart and my mind forever.
(And forgive us, o furious father, for the damage to the pocket.)

Sour Puss

You caught me in the act
of making some sense of the world.
Every now and again it would happen,
every now and again there'd be
light through the window,
and sentences, as if by some miracle,
would be built to be understood...
Most times though, a thin haze of resentment
would fall between, and I would be
dragging my feet, head bowed,
along this uneven pavement.

Leave Me Alone

Leave me to talk to those people that I knew.
I missed my chance when they were still alive.
Now, sifting through papers and memories,
I conjure them again, and they are so happy to see me,

Walking more quickly than I remembered,
Dodging every one of life's calamities,
From the Zeppelin that fell on the neighbour's street,
To that gas main explosion which left her hairless and grinning.

How could so much have happened to so few?
And how did I miss it when I could have shared it all?
Why was I so busy with my own important affairs
When they were reared over me like monuments to be ignored?

The Accident

I'm going to measure you
by the pencil stubs
you've left in this tray,
the fat ones and the short ones,
the ones you abandoned because
you had no further use for them that day.

I'll borrow them if I may
and finish off the picture
you were making that morning
when you just popped out for something
and never apparently saw
what was coming your way.

Something Precious

Sometimes I just want to go away
and stick my head under a pillow -

when it's raining on a Saturday, for example,
when everything should have been lovely,

and I'd be walking round the market building,
bird-spotting, amongst the records in Woollies,

looking out for a glance back
when I glance across,

and even thinking of
buying something precious.

Blackpool Promenade

I love the sea, the way it goes on and on.
You don't have to go in.
You can just get your toe end wet

like papa does,
when he pulls up his trouser leg,
and goes *ooh eck!*

an' everybody's
standing round and laughing.
I wish Blackpool were forever and a day.

The Dangers of Blackpool Rock

You can break your milk tooth
on a stick of Blackpool rock.
I did once.

It took ages to get it off,
it's so gluey.
The dentist held it up

to show me - half a front tooth stuck
to a chunk of red and white stripey rock.
That'll learn you, my lad, he said,

about sweet stuff, the dangers,
as he popped it into
a dinky plastic bag.

I sucked it to nothing later
(not the tooth bit).
Delicious.

Hope

Where did you say you were from?
I've never been there myself.
I wouldn't fancy it one bit.
Too much smoke.
Too many folks.

How long have you been here then?
You've lots to be finding out
if you haven't heard her talking.
She'll be gassing away at you
till Monday morning.

Walking Through Days

Folks didn't walk to go anywhere.
They just did it for the sake of it,
for a bit of fresh air,
or to see what was going on
when the street was empty.

They looked happy enough
when they got back home.
They'd fall into a chair,
lift one leg over another,
and tap out a fag from the packet.

That was what you did with days.
They just slipped away,
one after another:
a walk, a smoke,
nowt much to be said,
trying to avoid overmuch bother.

All the Time in the World

Should I wait here on this corner
now it's raining?
You never said you'd be later
than you said you'd be.
It's getting to be a bit of a
maddening habit,
me waiting here, kicking my heels,
and you sauntering along, all dolled up,
when you're good and ready,
as if there were all the time in the world
between now and next Christmas.
If you didn't turn on that smile each time,
I might just not stand it.
Girls, I ask you.

Middle-aged bachelor in profile at the window

You're farther away now
than I ever thought you'd go.
Usually it was just down to the shops
for a bit of polony,
or off to the chemists
for cod liver oil and malt
when I felt a bit seedy
and couldn't do owt but
maunge around this kitchen table.

Now you've been gone for longer,
and I don't know what to do with
all this upsetness
that keeps coming over me.
The medicines are still here
in their stoppered bottles,

but I get so mixed up
about the dosage.
You'd better come back soon
with that copper spoon
from my metal-work class at school
still brimming over.
I can't seem to cope, mum,
with all this fuss and bother.

Big Girls

Some of the girls are just
too big for my liking.
They're too noisy an all,
like fog horns blaring.

I like the smaller ones
with the quiet voices,
the ones who don't run at you
in the playground,
pretending not to notice.

Big girls take up too much space
in the classroom.
They always know what's what,
even when they don't.

I'm never going to love a girl
that's six inches taller than I am
in her stockinged feet.
I'm not partial
to being frowned down on.

What Gets You Going

Sooner or later,
if you wait around long enough,
you find out who you are
and what gets you going.

For me, it was darts in the pub
on a monday evening,
the way those feathers bristled
when they hit the board,

and then, quietly appraising
what went in and stayed put,
how you picked up that pint mug,
ever so slowly.

English Teacher walking up Barnsley Road, 1967

A stony, bookish man. A life apart
From all the other lives along that street.
A man in a black coat in summertime.
A man pernickety with single leaves.

A stary, bookish man, sparing of words.
A man who nodded when he thought to nod.
At other times, some studied sideways glance
At walls, flowers, trees. Or inward, to some god.

A bookish man, unneighbourly, tall, dour,
Who let his washing hang there, rain or shine.
A man forever walking through these parts,
Swinging a leather bag, shapeless with age.

The Pain of Separation

I never felt any pain of separation.
I just kept on going,
over bridges, through tunnels, along roads,
without even enquiring
whether they were your places.

I just knew that they were, all of them,
one by one, hour by hour, day by day,
and I was getting through,
numbed and painless, without you.
And it just went on and on and on.

What a bloody palaver is dead love.

Barretta Street (down Owler Lane way)

The cindery track through the allotments,
that was the place.
He never went down there again.
He just didn't feel partial to it.

Not that he couldn't still see it.
He saw it all the time,
when the lights were out,
and then, years later,
when he was just walking along
or buying food or talking, he'd see it again,
the way that lad raised his hand,
then brought it hard down.

He couldn't get rid of it.
Even when he got tall
and the lad stayed medium small

with that look of a ferret,
he couldn't bear to glance at him,
he couldn't stand to be
in the same world as him,
let alone have him living, life-long,

in the neighbouring street to theirs.

His Street

There were this street
we never went along
because *he* went along it,
dragging his feet,
with that dirty white muffler
tied round his neck
and that slouch cap
pulled at all angles
to cover his smutty face.

He allus came back from the works
down Brightside
at the same hour
an' his face was allus like stone,
set in this horrible scowl,
like he hated everybody.

So we just didn't go there, never,
and when he died -
summat wrong wi' his lungs -
we still didn't go there,
cos he were still there
even when he weren't there
for years an' years after.

Just Don't Try It

Who do you think you are
when you're at home?
Don't try that la-di-dah voice on me,
you jumped up nobody
from just off Burngreave Road..

The Best Necklace

The Christmas lights are all strung out
like mum's best necklace,
the one she wears at Christmas,

then keeps locked in this velvet box
for the next special occasion.
Once I opened it up just to look

before she could waltz in to stop me.
That necklace is so precious.
Nearly as precious as me, she once said, smiling.

Coach

I just can't fathom where we're going.
No one tells me owt.
It's a treat, they said, and then, pushin' me: climb in.

It's reyt stuffy in here.
There's sweat an' farts an' all sorts.
That lady who's not looking quite right's
just asked for a bag to be sick in...

I wish we could go back
and play out in the street
with bikes and stuff like that...

Ooh, look, there's the sea
Ovver there, winking at me!
We've arrived!

Mum, mum, are you listening?
It says on that big board
it's Great Yarmouth!

Girls Everywhere

There are girls everywhere,
in the church in the front pew,
at the back of the cinema,
with flickery eyelashes
and quiet little glances.
I want to squeeze one up against me.

There are girls everywhere.
There's my sister for example,
and her gobby mouth
around the kitchen table.
She threw the salt at me once.
I nearly kicked her.

There are girls everywhere.
I like the smaller ones,
the ones that don't run at you
and scare you,
the ones who don't just stand there,
hands on hips,
when you're queuing for school dinners.

Early Bird

I get out most days right early,
when the wind's keen,
and the kiddies are hell-for-leathering it
up the road to Hucklow Road Primary.

They're always late.
That's why they're in such a hurry.
Not me.
Me, I've got all the time in the world

to be seeing what's what -
who's carrying their bread back from Gregory's -
with two ounces of potted meat please
in greaseproof paper -

who's fresh buried.

Not a Word

No word of apology.
Why should she?
When you're right,
everybody else's allus wrong.
Stands to reason.

So she walks off -
flounces off more like -
down the gennel,
mouth set,
heels clicking.

Good riddance
to bad rubbish.

Laughter

Laughter's got
a lot of explaining to do.
It seldom gets it.

That time you laughed fit to bust
with the ice cream cone in your fist,
wobbling the cold slop of it into your hankie,

or when Frankie Howerd came on
and tipped you the wink,
so brazen, so saucy.

You couldn't stop yourself then.
You made the whole front row
of those pricey best seats tremble.
My sister's the same.
When she laughs,
she brings the whole ceiling
down with her.

Or as good as.
It's a sort of infection,
I reckon.

What's It All About Then?

What is it all meant to mean
when all's said and done?
Don't ask me.
I'm just the neighbour.

Where did she go to
when she took her hook?
Over there somewhere, I reckon,
down that gennel,
though I couldn't say for sure
because I didn't exactly know her.

Why did you lie to me
when I asked you point blank?
I have no idea.
I don't know what got into me.
I must have been off with the fairies -
or some such rubbish.

Greyhound Racing at Poole Road

Who needs money when words will do?
Words have taken me to such places in my life -
the War Memorial at Barker's Pool,
up Grenoside way to sniff at the air,
down to the dog track without a thought of a flutter.
Words are such weapons to be wielding
that I keep them strapped here, tight to my chest.
And only I know when to deploy them.

Biding His Time

He just stands there,
staring at nothing,
fag on, chipping
his toe end, waiting.

The chippy smell's gorgeous.
They slip in and out
with their bundles in newspapers
faster than you can count them.

But what's *he* there for?
Nobody knows him.
His hair's all mussed up.
There's no bus stop nearby.

Next time I check on him,
he's gone though,
with not a soul to ask
where to, chum.

Just Not Noticing

I'm here all the time.
You just haven't noticed.
You stopped noticing years back
if the truth were told.

We're like old wallpaper now, us.
We just don't see each other.
We go through the motions only -
gardening, tinkering with
that back door lock.
The only folk you smile at
are on the television.

Gormless

I walked only as far as the shops.
You grant me that, don't you?
And then I came back.
Fifteen minutes top whack!

Why then do you fret and say
you lost me for the whole, live-long day
when all I was doing
was catching up with some shopping?

Are you wet or daft or what?
Or do you spend too much time gazing at screens,
and never look truth in the eye
in the form of me?

All-Talk

He came back, did All-Talk.
All day he laid it down,
that big bloke, flinging out his arms,
waiting to be listened to.

All-Talk, he blethered on –
no one thought to talk him down –
statue-still or prancing round.
The know-hows get the audience.

All-Talk, I see him still,
now we're stamping on his grave,
up and down, across and round,
the last laugh's ours on All-Talk.

Emily

She's not all there, love,
my mother said,
tightening her grip on my hand,
thinking I'd be scared,
before we went in.
I wasn't.
She was right though.
She was old and she was young,
both at once.
She never stood up.
She never spoke.

Her skin was smooth and pale as a plate.
Her eyes shone, but at no one.
She blew little bubbles as if it were a game.
When her mum fed her,
she pushed the spoon through her lips,
that were limp and blubbery,
as if she couldn't hold them together.
Lots of food got left behind.

The only time she grinned
was when I took her hand.
You should have felt that grip!
Let him go, love, he's got to leave now,
her mum had to say -
mouthing directly into her face - eventually.

She was Emily, I think.

Kiddies

Kiddies run back and forth,
forth and back, never stopping.
They know what's what, do kiddies.
Until they're fagged out,
and then they just flop.

Into beds.
Onto chairs, park benches or carpets.
When a kiddie's quiet like that,
it's hard to believe
he/she's the same small person.

Revenge

Answer me this then.
Are little kids with posh voices
better or worse than
great big kids with loud voices?

Little kids don't punch you.
They're too freet for that.
They sneer instead,
small words through thin lips.

Big kids knock you about no end,
but you get your own back in the end.
When they want a job,
being desperate dads far too young,

you just say no
when Thelma asks you in the office
if they're any good at
chucking stuff about warehouses.

Losing the Winking Kind

Not in the way you once said it would be
when I first asked you.
Not like that at all.
Now you want your bread
buttered on both sides,
And I'm not having any of it.
Do you get me?

Where has all that sweet talk gone?
Where's that girl
that once stood on that corner,
one leg drawn back, saucy,
pointy shoe pointing straight down,
winking straight back at me?
That didn't happen very often.
Girls aren't usually the winking kind.
You were then.

You're not like that now though.
Now you're like a whirring machine
that just goes on and on,
same old stuff all day long.
Thank god there's some fresh air
on the other side of that window.

What It's Come Down to...

This is what it's
come down to then -
my word against yours
on a filthy morning,
with buckets catching the drips,
two heavy colds between us,
and enough food in the larder
to feed a tom tit.

Sheffieldish

When the street loses its dignity, each cobble stone begins to question its place in the world. These houses have been broken apart by war and human misery, a little helping of both for good cheer's sake. Pull the other one, mate.

Back-to-back, as if tied together for all eternity. Or dumped in Hell's river, two enemies, inseparable. For all eternity. Or to listen at the walls to all those whisperings of hatred: who left the corpse of a dead cat inside that bin? Who clatter-banged the lid in the night? There's no sleep to be had, is there, and no relaxation, when the walls hang so thin between friends-cum-enemies...

The art of toe-scuffing in best shoes, to knock off the shameful shine of newness or give a bit of street rowdiness to what would otherwise walk so straight and so tight and so face-scrubbed-clean - at a funeral, say, or, worse, some hateful wedding down at St Cuthbert's, with dandruff confetti chucked just for the sake of it, an' at anyone!

God's not anywhere where smoke is because smoke is too dirty and it gets on your clothes, and it makes you think filthy thoughts, filthy as chimney smoke curly-whirling up to the gold gates of heaven, then even filthier and more ragged still. Smoke gets in your eyes until the entire world is black as stinking, new laid asphalt down the street being steam-rollered. Ovver Fat Gut's toes an' all if he's not sharpish.

I said all those names out loud to myself as if they were gluey with sex and lust and seminal fluid: Nether Edge, Ecclesall, Brightside, Fir Vale, Pitsmoor. I dug in deep there, warming to my lubricious game: Totley Rise, Handsworth, Wincobank, and, oh, The Moor - more of that! - and even (oh my) Owler Bar. I was lying there on my back in bed, all done in, by the end. Did you ever find me there, dead happy? Had you had a right good time down the Sunbeam, mum, that Thursday, with Robert Mitchum?

He just stood there and said nowt just as if there were nowt to say. So we shoved him a bit an' he still said nowt. And then Paxo whacked him. That were when it all went ape-shit, that afternoon on Wincobank Hill, which had started out so sunny an' all. And all ovver a couple of drippin' sandwiches.

There's six of us here, in this steamy little pot of a house. We keep colliding. All the places we want to visit are allus locked from the inside, with the same voices calling out: wait your flippin' hurry!

I want you to drippin' my bread because you have such a way with the side of the knife, smoothin' it from side to side so thickly, and never failing to spread around those thin, brown streaks of gravy. So yummy. Will you promise to do it forever? Only kiddin'. There's so much finger jabbin' in this house and only so much bread to go around.

I'm not what you think I am.
In fact, I'm you today,
Smart-arsin' through every exam,
Quick-tickin' all the black boxes.

There's light at the far end of this gennel of ours, an entire world to burst out into, with sunlight and sky and smoke and shops lit up for your pennies, and botheration from just about everyone who never knew you and all those who did an' all. And that's only for starters.

Endgame

Palliative Care Ward at the Northern General Hospital

She's a right article that one,
with her bits of shawls round her shoulders!
My mother tut-tutted.
She couldn't have been more disgusted.

Her head looked as small as a pea
bundled up inside that giant purple cardigan of hers
she'd knitted for keeping out the cold.

She'd laughed when she'd said those words.
She just knew when she was being comical.

She couldn't stop herself calling
visitors to the opposite bed,
even when her own life was nigh on going going gone.

Saying Goodbye to Mother

The last breath is the only breath.
There beside you. A small flurry of the fingers.
The last smile is the only smile.
Shawls heaped about your shoulders.

The last word is the only word.
Look after yoursen, love. Get enough to eat.
Dying away. The long, last walk.
There's loads of food in t' freezer.

The last look is the only look.
So shrunken-small beneath the blankets.
Larger than life through the eyes of a child become man.
Small. Smaller. Nothing.

City Road Cemetery, Sheffield

She died. Why? Then they went to bed.
The cushions sprawled about the chairs.
I couldn't seem to find a bulb.
Folks drifted by. Ay, mum's the word.

When morning broke, I locked that door.
The milk were asking to come in.
I found this hat that didn't fit.
Our Arthur said: gi' us that bin.

On Tuesday week, the three of us –
her two best friends had wanted to –
remarked on how dull weather looks
above an urban cemetery.

Safely Elsewhere
i.m. Dorothy Alice Gladys Glover (1916-2009)

I scribble on this wall of broken promises.
I pick about this heap of fanciful dropped flowers.
You are not here to see me doing any of this.
You have signed off. You are already in another place.

My pen is driven by the energy of your voice.
But when you arrive, you also disappear.
I know you will not be wiping your feet on this mat by the door.
I know not to expect you any more.

There is nothing settled about any of this.
It's all flounderings, smudgings, the wildest swings of the bat.
And yet you still stand, chuntering, somewhere near.
You are here even when you are not here.

I write on this wall of broken promises.
I write words as true as words can ever be.
You are not here to see me doing any of this.
You have signed off.

You are already safely in another place.

Dorothy and I on Wincobank Hill

Where is she then, my mother? The house is rubbed away,
chalk from a blackboard. Where it once stood,
on solid ground, I now stand...

I look up at Wincobank Hill again,
rising up over the terraces,
never so engulfed by trees back then as it is these days.

She would have marvelled at it.
Now, once again, I take her there.
Up we go, arm in arm, to see old Sheffield in the raw...

climbing past dwarf oaks to the near bald, treeless summit,
seeing over to where those Don Valley chimneys still spew out
flame and smoke pother across smutty Templeborough...

Really? No, not really. All gone, all gone...As is she,
I remind myself, gently letting go of her arm.
These days young trees up Wincobank way have taken over.

About the author

Michael Glover was born in Sheffield. He is currently Poetry Editor of the *Tablet* and a senior art critic and a feature writer for the *Independent*. He has been a regular reviewer and commentator upon the world of poetry for the *Economist*, the *New Statesman* and the *Independent*. He has written about poetry in performance for the *Financial Times*. In 2009 he established *The Bow-Wow Shop*, a free-to-access, online poetry magazine which has been archived by the British Library.

What other poets and critics have said about Michael Glover's poetry:

'Much energy and brio' - Seamus Heaney, Nobel Prize in Literature, 1995

'Michael Glover's lines unspool gravely and efficiently with few commas - like waves that know they are on their way to someplace, but without making much fuss about it. They can be piercingly sad and hilariously wry, sometimes at the same time. Michael Glover is a major find.' - John Ashbery

'Michael Glover gives us, often dazzlingly, the poet as performer, conjuror, clown, operating with a playfulness which, whether putting forward arguments about language, reality or poetry itself, is artful and frequently highly enjoyable.' - Laurence Sail, *Stand*

'Enviably idiosyncratic and, for that reason, attractive' - Joseph Brodsky, Nobel Prize in Literature, 1987

'Michael Glover, journalist, critic and poet, writes with clarity, wit and, best of all, he makes sense of non-sense.' - Barry Fantoni, co-founder, *Private Eye*

www.ingramcontent.com/pod-product-compliance
Lightning Source LLC
Chambersburg PA
CBHW061730070526
44583CB00024B/3073